Pebble®
Plus

Monkeys

Capuchin Monkeys

by Cecilia Pinto McCarthy

Consulting Editor: Gail Saunders-Smith, PhD

Consultant: Lori Perkins,
Vice President of Collections
Zoo Atlanta, Atlanta, Georgia

CAPSTONE PRESS
a capstone imprint

Pebble Plus is published by Capstone Press,
1710 Roe Crest Drive, North Mankato, Minnesota 56003
www.capstonepub.com

Library of Congress Cataloging-in-Publication Data
Cataloging-in-publication information is on file with the Library of Congress.
ISBN 978-1-62065-108-7 (library binding)
ISBN 978-1-4765-1079-8 (ebook PDF)

Editorial Credits
Christopher L. Harbo, editor; Bobbie Nuytten, designer; Svetlana Zhurkin, media researcher;
Eric Manske, production specialist

Photo Credits
Alamy: Tom Stack Assoc./Ross, 21; iStockphotos: Damian Evans, cover, 1, Jeremiah Deasey, 7, vilainecrevette, 9, Ziga Camernik, 13; Minden Pictures: Pete Oxford, 5; Nature Picture Library: Pete Oxford, 15; Shutterstock: Helen E. Grose, 19, Ivan Kuzmin, 17, Kjersti Joergensen, 11

Note to Parents and Teachers

The Monkeys set supports national science standards related to life science. This book describes and illustrates capuchin monkeys. The images support early readers in understanding the text. The repetition of words and phrases helps early readers learn new words. This book also introduces early readers to subject-specific vocabulary words, which are defined in the Glossary section. Early readers may need assistance to read some words and to use the Table of Contents, Glossary, Read More, Internet Sites, and Index sections of the book.

Printed in the United States of America in North Mankato, Minnesota.
092012   006933CGS13

Table of Contents

Clever Monkeys

Smash! A capuchin cracks

a nut with a stone.

Capuchins are smart monkeys.

They make tools from stones,

sticks, and other objects.

Say It Like This:
Capuchin: kuh-POO-chin

5

Twelve kinds of capuchins live
in Central and South America.
They spend most of their lives
in the treetops.

where capuchins live

Capuchin Bodies

Capuchins are covered

in brown and black fur.

Many have cream-colored faces.

Some capuchins have fuzzy

tufts on their heads.

Adult capuchins are the size
of human newborn babies.
They have long, strong tails.
Capuchins use their tails to
balance on branches.

Tufted Capuchin
18 inches
(46 centimeters)

6 feet
(183 cm)

Finding Food

Capuchins eat figs, berries, nuts, eggs, and insects. Capuchins that live near water hunt crabs and oysters.

Growing Up

Female capuchins give birth
to one baby every two years.
As the baby grows stronger,
it rides on its mother's back.

Capuchins are fully grown
by age one.

Around age seven, males join
new capuchin groups.

Capuchins live about 25 years.

Living Together

Capuchins move about in
troops of five to 25 monkeys.
They play and groom together.
Grooming keeps fur clean and
helps capuchins bond.

Capuchins whistle loudly to warn of danger from snakes, jaguars, and harpy eagles. They make sounds to communicate and stay together.

Glossary

balance—to keep steady and not fall over

bond—to form a close friendship with someone

communicate—to pass along thoughts, feelings, or information

groom—to clean and keep neat

newborn—recently born

oyster—a flat shellfish that lives in shallow coastal waters; oysters have shells made of two hinged parts

troop—a group

tuft—a bunch of fur

warn—to tell about a danger that might happen in the future

whistle—to make a high, loud sound by blowing air through your lips

Read More

Aloian, Molly and Bobbie Kalman. *Endangered Monkeys*. Earth's Endangered Animals. New York: Crabtree Pub. Co., 2007.

Owen, Ruth. *Mischievous Monkeys*. Eye to Eye with Animals. New York: Windmill Books, 2012.

Riggs, Kate. *Monkeys*. Seedlings. Mankato, Minn.: Creative Education, 2012.

Internet Sites

FactHound offers a safe, fun way to find Internet sites related to this book. All of the sites on FactHound have been researched by our staff.

Here's all you do:

Visit *www.facthound.com*

Type in this code: 9781620651087

Super-cool stuff! Check out projects, games and lots more at
www.capstonekids.com

23

Index

Word Count: 185
Grade: 1
Early-Intervention Level: 16